Garden Memories

Garden Memories

The Minnesota Landscape Arboretum
By
Robert Pickering Sr.

BSM Publishing
Minneapolis, Minnesota

Garden Memories
The Minnesota Landscape Arboretum
Copyright © 2019 by Robert Pickering Sr.
Second Edition

Photos by Robert Pickering Sr.
Maps supplied by Arboretum staff.

Printed in the United States of America

First Printing 2019
ISBM **978-0-9883074-5-2**

BSM Publishing
12000 Marion Lane, #1101
Minnetonka, MN 55305-1302

This is for all who have contributed, year after year, to making the Minnesota Landscape Arboretum a beautiful community asset. Thank you for the joy you bring to so many.

Acknowledgements

Steve Rossi, my editor, designer, teacher and friend who generously assists me in my writing efforts.

The Minnesota Landscape Arboretum staff for creating and maintaining our source of content..

Contents

Garden Memories

The Minnesota Landscape Arboretum, a University of Minnesota horticultural research facility in Chaska, Minnesota, has over twenty-five named gardens, Three Mile scenic walk and drive, a Bee and Pollinator research center, farm and walking trails through forests, bogs, and meadows. In this 2024 edition, my wife June and I share our memories of the gardens.

The view from the Snyder Building toward the Oswald Visitor Center.

Spring in the Garden

Azaleas and Lilacs
abound.

The Lilac Walk and Collection are special places in spring.

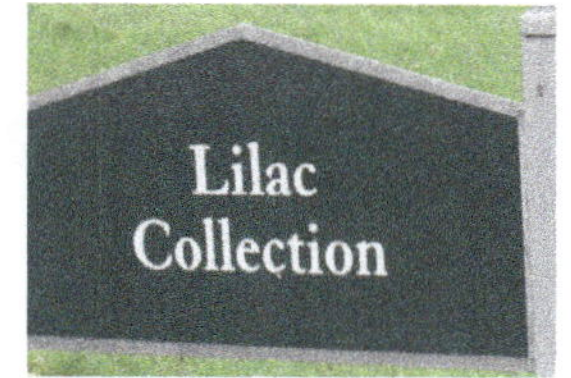
Lilac
Collection

The Arboretum staff and volunteers plant over 75,000 bulbs to insure a beautiful spring.

Along the parking lots near the Oswald Visitor Center with daffodils, tulips and hyacinth.

Daffodils next to a sunny bench.

Over 35,000 tulips in spring.

Thousands of daffodils.

Oswald building entrance.

Azaleas

Tulips and hyacinths.

Magnolia trees in full bloom along
Three Mile Drive near the steps to
the Shrub Rose and Maze Gardens.

Iris Garden

A purple rhododendron with its blossom.

An April White Rhododendron

Spring flowers attract
bees.

Rhododendron Garden

The Shrub Walk on Three Mile Drive fills with the color of Rhododendrons, Azaleas and Lilacs.

Pink Magnolia Blossom

Forsythia

Crabapple
Collection

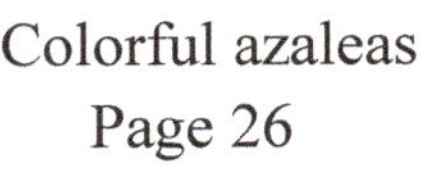
Colorful azaleas
Page 26

Beautiful Peonies

Summer in the Garden

Oswald Visitor Center entrance area

The landscaping between buildings.

Snyder walk...

...and garden.

Page 32

A walk between the Oswald and Snyder buildings brings you to the Terrace Garden, a great place to start your garden tour.

Tasteful art with
a background of
trees.

The walk to the main garden from the terrace has color from spring through the fall.

Water features are flowing as we come to the Dwarf Conifer and Kitchen Herb Gardens.

Dwarf Conifers

Kitchen Herb Garden

Lily Collection

Annual Garden

Annual Garden

Summer beauty and color.

Beautiful paths and fountains.

Ants, bees and frogs

Rose Walk

Across the Road

A focus on roses

Across the road are a variety of gardens
.

To the left of Three Mile Drive the Rose Garden displays roses, a gazebo, fountains enclosed by lattices covered with blossoms.

The Sensory and Wildflower gardens are down the hill.

On the right of Three Mile Drive the Rock Garden is situated at the entrance to the Japanese garden with its water features and tea house.

Following the path on the left is the Home Demonstration Garden with plants you will recognize from your dining table, a koi pond water feature in the Woodland Azalea Garden. The path goes through the Hosta Glade to the Fern Walk past a pond behind Behren's cabin.

Rosa
'WEKlurk'
Dick Clark
2011 AARS Grandillora Rose

Rosa
'WEKjuvoo'
Chris Evert®
Hybrid Tea Rose

Surrounded by lattice covered with color!

Across the garden the gazebo is surrounded with roses and fountains.

The Rock Garden

Japanese Garden entrance and tea house.

Water feature and Koi.

A learning place!

The Woodland Azalea Garden

Hundreds of hostas in a shaded glade amongst a forest of maples and oaks. These woods are quiet and beautiful.

The path leads to ferns and a pond behind Behren's cabin.

The Fern walk connects
with Three Mile Drive
behind Behren's cabin
past a still pond with
tasteful art work.

Artful fish!

The Sensory Garden
Restore, Relax, Renew
Calling All Senses

Gardens on Three Mile Drive

The Johanna Frederich Garden for Wildlife

A half mile educational walk of beauty shared with wildlife.

Monarchs and Turkeys

Examples of habitat across the bridge.

Meadows, berries and flowers for habitat.

Grapes, black choke ber-
ries and cranberries feed
wildlife.

Shrub Walk

Shrub roses decorate the entrance.

Harrison Sculpture Garden

The sculpture garden is on over three acres of rolling hills surrounding the Arboretum's High point. The art works interplay with a landscape of open countryside that changes with every season.
The sculptures were generously donated by philanthropists Ingrid Lenz Harrison and Alfred Harrison of Wayzata.
University of Minnesota Landscape Arboretum (2018, November 18. Retrieved from http://www.arboretum.umn.edu/sclupture_garden.aspx)

Confluence 1991
Antione Poncet
Rose Marble

Stone Harp 1993
Rene Kung
Limestone

Swimmers 1990
Paul T Granlund
Bronze

Stone Arch 1995
Rene Kung
Limestone

Rolling Over 1963
F E McWilliam
Bronze

Canto Notturno 1984
Mimmo Paladino
Bronze

Night Gesture 1976
Louise Nevelson
Welded Aluminum

Roses and statues everywhere!

Dahlia Trial Garden
Winterberry Collection

The Chinese Garden

Hydrangea Test Area

The Maze Garden

Tall Grasses

Family
Douglas Olmstad Freeman

BSM Publishing

BSM is a publishing company founded by June and Bob Pickering to raise money for gardens visited over fifty years of touring. The 2019 editions are photo tours of the Minnesota Landscape Arboretum in Chaska, Minnesota. Enjoy them!

Trees on Three Mile Drive
Seventy plus scenes photographed along Three Mile Drive featuring a specific tree in each view.

East Side Trails
The east side of the Arboretum contains bogs, swamps, ponds and meadows that are representative of Minnesota's great outdoors. We guide you on a photo tour of this wonderful area.

Garden Memories
A photo tour of the many garden areas in and about the Arboretum. There are twenty-seven named gardens on the Arboretum tour map.